こども歌舞伎

長浜曳山まつり

ユネスコ無形文化遺産登録

写真　吉川宏暉

長浜曳山まつり

（公財）長浜曳山文化協会　理事　西川丈雄

はじめに

長浜曳山まつりは、長濱八幡宮の祭礼として例年四月十五日を中心に、多彩な行事をともなっておこなわれます。漆塗りや錺金具、懸装幕などで飾られた豪華な曳山とその舞台で演じられる子ども狂言（歌舞伎）は、この祭りの見どころであり、長浜の人々の誇りとなっています。また、子ども役者たちと役者を支える若い衆、曳山を守り行事を執行する中老、それを見守り支える家族や地域の人々、さらには観客たちとのつながりがみられる祭りでもあります。このような歴史と文化を伝える曳山祭は、「長浜曳山祭の曳山行事」として、昭和五十四年二月、国の重要無形民俗文化財に指定され、平成二十八年十一月三十日に「山・鉾・屋台行事」の一つとして全国三十二か所の祭りとともにユネスコ無形文化遺産に登録されました。

長浜曳山まつりの始まり

祭礼の由来書によれば天正元年（一五七三）、織田信長から浅井氏の旧領を与えられた羽柴秀吉が、琵琶湖岸に長浜城を築き、城下町を整備し、八幡宮の復興をはかりました。祭礼日を九月十五日と定め、長濱八幡宮創建に関わった八幡太郎義家（源義家）の凱旋の様子にちなんだ「太刀渡」をおこない、町年寄十人衆に継承させました（江戸時代なって十人衆が減少したため、長刀組がつとめることになりました）。

次いで、秀吉に男児が生まれたとき、長浜の町人たちは振舞われた祝い金をもとに曳山を造り、祭礼に曳いたことで、曳山まつりが始まったと伝えられています。こうして鎧武者の渡る歩行渡りに曳山の渡り、それに子ども狂言が加わり、さらにいろんな行事が整えられ、今日あるような特色のある長浜曳山まつりの形が江戸時代に整えられていきました。

江戸時代の長浜町

長浜曳山まつりの発展には、長浜町が秀吉以来の長浜町屋敷年貢米三百石の免除の朱印地、彦根藩の「町方」支配地であったことや長浜湊が彦根三湊の一つとして保護されたことなどがあげられます。

また、江戸時代中期からは浜糸（生糸）に加えて、浜縮緬、浜蚊帳、浜ビロードの生産が始まり、彦根藩の保護を受け、産物の生産・集散の地、北国街道の宿場町、琵琶湖舟運の湊町、湖北の真宗拠点長浜御坊大通寺や長濱八幡宮の門前町という多様な性格を併せもつ長浜五十二ヵ町（約千三百戸前後、人口約四千八百人前後）であったことでした。町人たちの曳山まつりへの思いは、まちの賑わいの象徴としての思いとともに現在にも脈々と受け継がれています。

曳山と子ども狂言・しゃぎり

成立当時の曳山の規模などは不明ですが、江戸時代には、新しい山になったり、亭の建造がされたり、見送幕・錺金具・彫刻等の装飾品の新調など町人たちによって整備され、現在のような曳山となりました。

「やま（曳山）」は十三基ありますが、太刀と幟を飾る長刀山以外の十二基は、曳山狂言を行う「やま」です。曳山は、全国的にも芸能を行う屋台として洗練された形式をしており、舞台・楽屋・花道を設け、しかも上部には趣向を凝らした楼閣造りの「亭（ちん）」が設けられています。亭は囃子の「しゃぎり」の演奏場所となっています。舞台では六、七歳から十一、二歳の男の子が可憐に曳山狂言（子ども歌舞伎）を演じます。

曳山狂言は、長浜では「山の芸」・「芸」とも呼ばれており、寛保二年（一七四二）の本教（台本）や明和六年（一七六九）からの外題記録によって、江戸時代中期にはすでに行われていたことがわかります。その後、天保の改革による江戸、京都、大阪の三都以外の歌舞伎風禁止により、一時、能狂言が行われてはいま

3

すが、概して歌舞伎狂言を主流にして演じられてきています。現在、十二の山組の四山組ずつが交代で、出番山となって狂言を仕組んで出場し、芸を競っています。また、曳山まつりの進行にしたがって演奏される囃子は「しゃぎり」と総称し、曲目は「御遣り」「神楽」「奉演間」「戻り山」「獅子」「鶴の巣ごもり」「起し太鼓」など二十数曲を伝承しています。

曳山祭の保存と伝承

曳山祭の保存伝承については、長刀組をはじめ各山組、保存団体の公益財団法人長浜曳山文化協会、その拠点・長浜市曳山博物館、長濱八幡宮と氏子、七郷、長浜曳山祭囃子保存会、市民や企業等の参加した長浜曳山祭協賛会、長浜観光協会そして行政関係などが協力しあって、保存伝承に努めています。近年はボランティアの参加、三役修業塾による振付・太夫・三味線の三役の養成、囃子保存会による子どもから大人の演奏後継者の育成、曳山の保存修理などもおこなわれてきていますが、少子高齢化や人口減少のなか、行事を運営する山組の維持、中老や若連中の後継者確保の方策も課題になっています。いずれにしても国の指定やユネスコ無形文化遺産となったことを契機にさらなる知恵を絞り努力をして、次の世代へと伝統あるこの曳山祭を伝えていくことは大きな責務といえます。

Origin of the festival

The Nagahama Hikiyama festival started about 450 years ago, during the Azuchi -Momoyama era (1573 - 1603), in Japan.

In 1573, the feudal warlord Hideyoshi Toyotomi had not only built the castle and its town, but also made an effort to reconstruct Nagahama Hachimangu. The shrine, one of the most important in Nagahama, was destroyed by fire in the Warring States period(1467 - 1591).

When Hideyoshi Toyotomi's male heir was born, he was so delighted that he gifted the people of the town a large sum of gold for celebration. It is said that from this gift of gold, the first Hikiyama Festival floats were made and paraded around the town and Nagahama Hachimangu.

The highlights of this festival are the luxurious floats and the Kabuki plays performed upon the stage on top of them by male children from the area. Since Hideyoshi built Nagahama castle, the city flourished as a commercial center for the area. Due to the financial prosperity and the gold received from Hideyoshi, the town people were able to dedicate a great amount of wealth to commissioning 12 different elaborate floats from skillful craftsmen of the time. Meanwhile, it is not clear when the Kabuki plays were incorporated into the festival, however some historical documents say it was already taking place between 1764 and 1772. The town people prepare for this festival for a couple of months and the festival is held for 9 days.

It is no exaggeration to say that Nagahama Hikiyama festival is one of the best festivals in Japan because of its splendidness and scale.

Since being registered by UNESCO as cultural heritage in 2016, it is believed that the popularity of this festival has been increasing globally.

曳山まつり行程表（目次）

通年	春休み	三月	三月	二月	二月	一〜三月	一〜二月	二月一日
三役修業塾	囃子稽古	稽古	稽古場作り	鬘・衣装合わせ	役者決め	パンフレット作り	若衆初寄り	山組集会
31	28	20	18	16	14	13	12	10

Mar	Decorating the floats	32
Apr 1	The general assembly of Yamagumi	34
Apr 1st Sat	Ceremony of switching out the floats to be used this year	35
	Parading the floats around town	38
Apr 9	Kabuki time keeping	42
Apr 9-12	"Naked" shrine visit	44
Apr 12	Ceremony of Mikoshi (a portable shrine) *Togyo	51
Apr 13	Taiko drum wake-up calls around the town	54
Apr 13	Ceremony of receiving *Gohei	56
Apr 13	Ceremony of casting lots for the order of Kabuki perfomances	60

*Gohei is a staff with plaited paper streamers which is used for Shinto ceremonies.
In Nagahama Hikiyama Festival, people believe that the god resides in the Gohei. It is set upon the float during the festival.
*Togyo is a transferral of a sacred object from its place of enshrinement.

四月十三日	四月十三日	四月十三日	四月十二日	四月九～十二日	四月九日		四月第一土曜日	四月一日	三月
くじ取り式	御幣迎えの儀	起こし太鼓	神輿渡御の儀	裸参り	線香番	曳山曳行	曳山交替式	総集会	山飾り
60	56	54	51	44	42	38	35	34	32

The schedule of Hikiyama Festival including the preparation

Feb 1	Yamagumi (Hikiyama float team) meeting	10
Jan-Feb	The first meeting of young members (22-45 years old)	12
Jan-Mar	Making brochures	13
Feb	Casting roles for the Kabuki performances	14
Feb	Wig and costume fitting	16
Mar	Building the training stage for the Kabuki performances	18
Spring holidays	Kabuki training for the children who will perform	20
All year around	Shagiri (Japanese traditional music) training	28
All year around	Juku for training Choreographer, Dayu, Syamisen	31

四月十五日	四月十五日	四月十五日	四月十五日		四月十四日	四月十四日	四月十四日十六日	四月十三日
狂言奉納	翁招き	長刀組太刀渡り	朝渡り	化粧・着付け	夕渡り	登り山	自町狂言	十三日番
93	92	90	87	81	75	69	65	64

Apr 15 Kabuki performance on the way to the Otabisho 102
Apr 15 Ceremonial Kabuki play dedicated to the gods of Nagahama Hachimangu at the Otabisho 103
Apr 15 Ceremony of Mikoshi kangyo, returning the Mikoshi to Nagahama Hachimangu 108
Apr 15 The festival floats going back to Nagahama Hachimangu 109
Apr 16 Public performance of Kabuki play at Nagahama Culture and Arts Hall 112
Apr 16 The last public Kabuki performance 113
Apr.17 Ceremony of returning the Gohei to Nagahama Hachimangu 117
       Cleaning up 119
       Afterword 122

四月十七日		四月十七日	四月十六日	四月十六日	四月十五日	四月十五日	四月十五日	四月十五日
あとがき	山片付け	御幣返しの儀	千秋楽	子ども歌舞伎観劇会	戻り山	神輿還御の儀	お旅所神前奉納	道中歌舞伎公演
122	119	117	113	112	109	108	103	102

Apr 13	Local Kabuki performances in each neighborhood	64
Apr 14&16	Kabuki play performance for their neighbors at their own town	65
Apr 14	Pulling the floats to the main shrine, Nagahama Hachimangu	69
Apr 14	Evening parade of child Kabuki actors in full costume	75
	Costume and make up	81
Apr 15	Morning parade of child Kabuki actors in costume	87
Apr 15	A samurai procession, Musha Gyoretsu by children	90
Apr 15	Opening ceremony for the festival	92
Apr 15	The Kabuki play dedicated to the gods of Nagahama Hachimangu	93

山組集会(二月一日)

総当番と長刀組はじめ十三山組の代表が長浜八幡宮で、その年の出番山組を確認、芸題が決まる

各山組の代表「負担人」たちは、長浜八幡宮に着いた順番に「着帳」に凡帳
Every "Futan-Nin", the representatives of their own teams, signs their name in the attendance book called "Chaku-Chou" as they arrive.

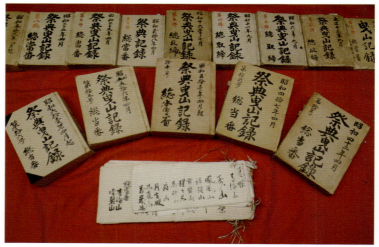

Yamagumi Syukai (February 1)

 *Soutou-Ban and representatives from the other 13 float teams, including Naginata-Gumi get together at Nagahama Hachimangu. They confirm the order and decide the titles of that year's Kabuki performances.

 *Soutou-Ban is the group with the highest authority for the festival. They decide the schedule and detailed rules for the proceedings that year. It consists of some "Churo" members of the float teams not responsible for Kabuki this year.

祭の総責任者「総当番委員長(手前右)」と座礼をかわす
The chairman of "Soutou-Ban", the group in charge of overseeing all the festival matters, and Futan-Nin exchange "zarei", a formal seated bow.

若衆初寄り（一〜二月）

役者係や舞台後見人など若衆の役割分担を決める。
いよいよ、祭が始まる

祭の成功を祈って乾杯
A toast to the success of the festival.

Wakasyu Hatsuyori (Jan-Feb)

They decide the roles, such as "Yakusha-Gakari", the caretaker for the child performers, and "Butai Kouken-Nin", the guardian of the stage. The festival preparations begin.

パンフレット作り（一〜三月）

出番山組が、写真を使いながら役者や芸題のあらすじ、行事などを紹介する。賛助広告をとってくるのも大切な仕事

最近では、英語の紹介も
Some parts of the festival brochure have recently started being translated into English.

Making brochures (Jan-Mar)

The float teams start making brochures that introduce the child Kabuki actors and the titles of their scheduled performances. It is also an important job for them to make the rounds to shops and businesses to sell advertisement space in the brochure.

役者決め(二月)

振付師が五~十二歳までの男児の年齢や体格、声質などを考慮し、適役を決める

振付師と子ども役者との初顔合わせ。保護者も緊張した面持ち
This is the first meeting between choreographer and child Kabuki actors. Their parents also look nervous.

役所がホワイトボードに
The names of the actors are written on a whiteboard.

早速、基本の歩き方を習う
Children start learning how to walk in the Kabuki style right away.

Yakusya Gime (February)

The Kabuki choreographer decides casting roles in the Kabuki play by considering the age, characteristics, and type of voice of the boys between 5 to 12 years old.

資料を見ながら慎重に役を決める振付師
The choreographer decides the casting by considering each child's characteristics.

鬘・衣装合わせ（二月）

鬘師が、子ども一人ひとりに合わせて鬘を作る。衣装の寸法を測る作業も

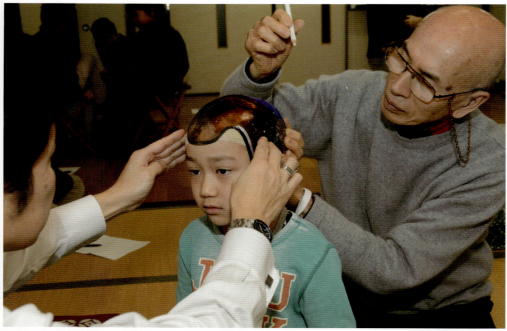

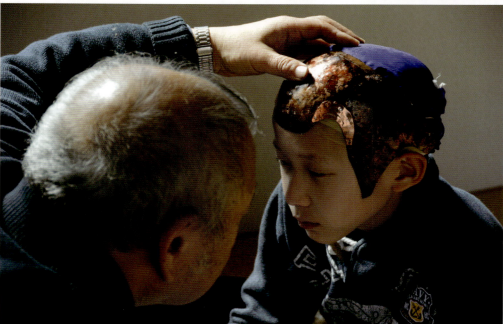

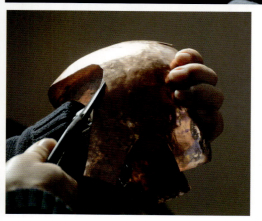

Katsura Isyou Awase (February)
A Kazura-shi, wig craftsman, makes wigs for each child Kabuki actor. And also we can see they are taking measurements for costumes.

稽古場作り(三月)

若衆らが町会館などに曳山の舞台とほぼ同じ大きさの仮舞台を設置、看板を立て稽古場を作る

Keikoba Dukuri (March)
In the community hall, young members of the team build the temporary stage for training which is almost same size as the real one. They also put up their team's sign.

提灯を点検する
They check paper lanterns to use during the procession.

稽古（春休み）

せりふの「読み習い」から始まり、所作を覚える立ち稽古に入る。朝、昼、夜の三回、厳しい稽古が続く

「読み習い」の稽古、夜まで続く
Children practice reading their lines late into the night.

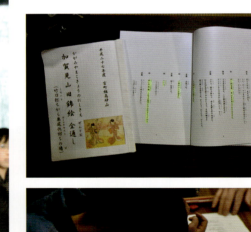

Keiko (Spring holidays-Mar-Apr)
From reading the lines, child actors start to rehearse and learn how to act. They endure hard training three times a day, morning, daytime and night until the day of the festival.

稽古を前に子ども役者の健康と祭りの成功を祈願
Before rehearsing the play, they pray for the children's health and success of the festival in front of the Gohei.

節回しを覚えながら
せりふの練習
A boy is reading his lines
while learning the proper
intonation.

「おなかに力を入れて」。
振付師の指導に力が入る
"Tighten your abdomi-
nals!", the choreographer
passionately instructs his
students.

せりふを覚えたら、立ち稽古へ
After memorizing the lines, they start rehearsing.

伊勢音頭恋寝刃　油屋

曳山博物館では「三番叟」の練習が続く
In the Hikiyama Museum, "Sanbaso", the opening act, continues to be rehearsed.

稽古の合間に卓球やゲームで
息抜き

Between rehearsals, there is time for recreation: playing table tennis and other games.

囃子稽古（通年）

長浜では「しゃぎり」と呼ぶ。篠笛、太鼓、摺り鉦（すりがね）で囃す。昔は口伝だったが、近年は採譜化された

曳山上部の「亭（ちん）」という狭い楼閣で囃す「囃子方」
"Sharigi-Gata", musicians who play the Japanese traditional music called "Shagiri", play in this narrow space up above the festival float, called "Chin".

Syagiri Keiko (All year)
　"Ohayashi" is a Japanese traditional orchestra consisting of flutes, drums, and bells. In Nagahama, they call it "Shagiri". In the old days, performers learned how to play it by oral instruction. But in later years, the melody has been written down in musical notation.

指導役の若衆の指使いを見ながら練習に励む子どもたち
Children watch the fingers of the instructor carefully, trying to learn how to play the flute.

囃子で祭りを支える
These girls play an important role in the festival by playing flute.

裸参りや曳山交替式などの行事にも参加
  Syagiri-Gata also take part in "Hadaka-Mairi", visiting the shrine naked, and alternation ceremony of festival floats.

三役修業塾

高齢化が心配されている振付、太夫、三味線の三役を地元で育てる長浜曳山文化協会の塾

Sanyaku Syugyo Juku

"Sanyaku" plays significant role in the Kabuki of the Nagahama Hikiyama Festival. It consists of three people, Furitsuke (the choreographer), Dayu (the narrator), and the Shamisen player. However, participants in the festival are worried that there are enough young people joining in the tradition. Sanyaku Shugyo Juku is a training school for raising the next generation in the local community supported by the Nagahama Hikiyama Cultural Association.(Nagahama Hikiyama Bunka Kyoukai)

山飾り（三月）

曳山の維持管理を担うのは「中老」の仕事。飾り幕や障子などを飾り付ける

Yama-Kazari (March)
 It's the "Churo", members of middle age in the float team, who are responsible for maintaining and taking care of the festival float. They decorate tapestries and Shoji (paper sliding doors) on the float.

曳山の舞台に初めて上がり、広さなどを確かめる子ども役者たち
The child actors get on the float for the first time to get familiar with its size.

曳山の後ろにつく「後山」(弁当山)を組み立てる長老たち
"Churo", middle aged members, assemble the float called "Atoyama (Bento-Yama)", which will follow after the festival float in the procession.

総集会（四月一日）

総寄りともいう。山組の代表らが、祭り全体の執行について最後の決定・確認をする

Yamagumi Sousyukai(April 1)
They call the assembly "Souyori". The representatives of all float teams get together in order to confirm and have the final decision about the whole execution of the festival.

曳山交替式（四月第一土曜日）

平成十一年に曳山博物館が開館したのを機に、祭りごとに十二基の曳山が四基交代で博物館に入る新しい行事

山蔵から曳き出されるその年出番の曳山
The float for this year's festival is being drawn out of the yamagura, its garage.

Hikiyama Koutai-Shiki (April 1st Saturday)
This is a new event started since the Hikiyama Museum was opened in 1999. Four out of 12 floats are alternately placed on public display in the museum every year.

曳山の中で唯一御座船型をした猩々丸には
陣羽織姿の「采振」が船首に立つ
The Shojo-Maru float is made to look like a noble's ship. It is the only float with a unique shape.

次年度、出番の曳山が博物館の山蔵に入る
The float for next year's festival is being drawn into the Hikiyama Museum.

曳山曳行

曳山交替式や登り山の時に、市内を曳行する

Hikiyama Eiko
The festival floats are pulled around the town during "alternation ceremony of the festival floats", "Nobori-Yama", and "Modori-Yama".

曳山の道中は昔ながらの狭い街並み、辻を曲がるのに一苦労
The float is struggling to turn a corner on a narrow street unchanged since olden times.

若衆が力いっぱい曳山を担ぐようにして方向転換
"Wakashu", young members of the float team, make a change of direction by carrying the float on their shoulders with all their might.

線香番（四月九日）

昔、線香の火（約四十分）で上演の長さを計ったことからこの名がついた。狂言が時間内に収まるように総当番が手分けして調べ回る

総当番が見守る中、緊張した面持ちで演技を披露
The children who have acted in Kabuki plays show solemn expressions in front of "Soutou-Ban".

Senko-Ban (April 9)

Since the old days, the method of timekeeping in Kabuki is by the fire of one incense stick. It takes almost 40 minutes to burn down, the same length as the whole performance of the play. That's the origin of the name, Senko-Ban.

Soutou-Ban goes around to check every float team to ensure it fits the performance into the correct time.

この日から一般に公開され、祭りムードが盛り上がる
The opening day of the Kabuki performances.

上演時間を確認する当番（左）
"Soutou-Ban" (left side) confirms the performance time of the plays with "Futan-Nin".

裸参り（四月九〜十二日夜）

若衆たちが、長浜八幡宮の井戸で水垢離をし、役者の健康と狂言奉納の順番を決める良い籤が引けるよう祈願する。豊国神社へも参る。

籤取り人を中心に出発前にお神酒で景気付け
They have a "Omiki", sacred sake to cheer up before leaving.

Hadaka-Mairi (April 9 to 12)

"Wakashu" pray for child actors' health and the good order of Kabuki play during the festival by performing "Mizugori", cold-water ablutions, at the well in Nagahama Hachimangu and Houkoku shrine.

いざ出陣。
水をかぶって気勢を上げる
"Let's get moving!".
Participants psyche themselves
up with cold water.

山組と山組がすれ違う。
緊張の一瞬
Two float teams are passing
each other. It's an intense
moment.

井戸の周りをかける若衆の提灯の火が大きく揺れ、風情を醸し出す
The flames of lanterns hoisted around the well by young people waver and flicker creating a poignant atmosphere.

水垢離のあと、本殿で祈願。厳かな雰囲気に包まれる
After Mizugori, cold water ablutions, they pray at Nagahama Hachimangu. The atmosphere is solemn.

「ヨイサ、ヨイサ」と勇ましい声が町中に響きわたる
"Yoisa, Yoisa.", their brave shout echoes all over the town.

借り衣装姿の子ども役者を抱き上げて健康を祈る
Young members lift the child actor in their arms and pray for their health.

冷えた体をストーブで温めながら、
地元の人たちの料理に舌鼓
They warm themselves by the heater
and enjoy delicious local food.

神輿渡御の儀（四月十二日）

長浜八幡宮から御旅所まで担がれる。十五日の狂言が終わるまで神輿堂に安置される

御神体を本殿から神輿に移す
Goshintai, the object of worship, is transferred from the inner shrine to the portable one.

神輿を厳粛な気持ちで迎える市民
On the street, we can see local people bowing reverently for the portable shrine with solemn expressions.

Mikoshi Togyo no Gi (April 13)

The portable shrine is carried from Nagahama Hachimangu to the "Otabisho".
It is placed in "Mikoshi-Do" by the 15th day until the public Kabuki performances are finished. The "Otabisho" is a place where the sacred palanquin is lodged during the festival.

道中、囃子に迎えられ御旅所へ向かう
On the way to the Otabisho, Hayashi is played for the portable shrine.

御旅所に着いた神輿は、神輿堂に安置される
After arriving at the Otabisho, the portable shrine is enshrined at Mikoshi-Do.

起こし太鼓（四月十三日未明）

「御幣迎え」のために笛や太鼓を囃しながら、祭礼関係者を起こし回る。十二の全山組が行う

Okoshi-Daiko (April 13)
For the ceremony of receiving the Gohei, all 12 of the float teams go around the neighborhood to wake up people involved in the festival by beating taiko drums and playing the flute.

起こし太鼓の途中、他の山組の稽古場を訪れ、気勢をあげる
During the taiko wake-up drumming, they visit the other float teams' training rooms, and encourage each other with drink.

御幣迎えの儀（四月十三日）

曳山に飾る御幣を長浜八幡宮へ迎えに行く。十三の全山組が参加する

Gohei Mukae no Gi (April 13)
They go to Nagahama Hachimangu to receive Gohei for placing on the float. All 13 float teams take part in the event.

持ち帰った御幣は御幣宿に預けられる
The received Gohei are kept in "*Gohei-Yado" during the festival.
 *Gohei-Yado is the family and its house who keeps the Gohei that year during the festival. A Shinto altar is set up in the house in which to place the Gohei.

狩衣烏帽子姿の御幣使が御幣を自町に持ち帰る
Gohei-Shi, a boy in *Kariginu costume with "eboshi" formal headwear, brings the Gohei back to his town.
 *Kariginu is an everyday-outfit for court nobles when hunting. It's has a more free feeling than formal dress.

鳥居の前では総当番が見送る
Soutou-Ban see the Gohei-Shi and the company off at the torii.
 *Torii is a shrine gate.

籤取り式(四月十三日)

狂言奉納の順番を決める籤を引く神事

引いた籤を披露する籤取り人。幣殿の外では、若衆たちが招き扇を振って励ます
Kujitorinin make the lottery in front of the people. The young members encourage Kujitorinin by waving Maneki-ougi, a kind of fortune fan.

Kujitori-Shiki (April 13)
 It's a Shinto ritual to draw for the order of Kabuki plays.

会食をして籤取りに備える
There is a dinner meeting before the Kujitori-Shiki, casting lots for turn order.

籤取り人を先頭に「ヨイサ、ヨイサ」と招き扇を振りながら長浜八幡宮へ
With a shout of "Yoisa", the Kujitorinin leads the company accompanied by waving Maneki-Ogi fans, all the way to Nagahama Hachimangu.

「良い籤がひけますように」
" Let our team get a good spot in order!"

鯉を長浜八幡宮の放生池に放つ山組も
Some groups release a carp into the pond at Nagahama Hachimangu to garner good fortune.

「籤取り」を終えた籤取り人を胴上げして喜ぶ
A Kujitorinin who finishes casting lots is tossed into the air by his teammates.

十三日番（四月十三日）
夕方から各山組の町内での狂言披露。
本衣装に鬘をつけ、初めての曳山の舞台

Juusannichi-Ban (April 13)
On the evening of the 13th, the performance of Kabuki plays can be seen in each town.
This is the first public performance in full traditional costume this year.

自町狂言（四月十四、十六日）
十四日の登り山の前に町内で披露。十六日は「後宴」として各山組の町内で一日数回、披露される

習熟した子ども役者の演技に振付け師も満足気
The choreographer looks satisfied with the skilled performances of the child actors.

Jimachi-Kyogen (April 14.16)

Before "Nobori-Yama", on the 14th day, the float teams perform in front of their neighbors, in their own town. On the 16th, as one of "*Goen", they have the public performance of Kabuki play in each float's town several times throughout the day.

"*Goen" is a general term including the Kabuki play on the 16th and in Culture and Arts Hall, Nagahama Bunka Geijyutsu Kaikan. If "Honbi", all events on the day of the 15th, are for the God in Nagahama Hachimangu and the sightseers, "Goen" events are for the local people.

演技を終えた子ども役者に観客から大きな拍手
Upon finishing the play, the children receive a big round of applause.

見物の園児に笑顔を見せる子ども役者
The Kabuki actors smile at the younger, kindergarten children.

ゲームしながら出番を待つ
Some children are killing time by playing video games while waiting their turn to perform.

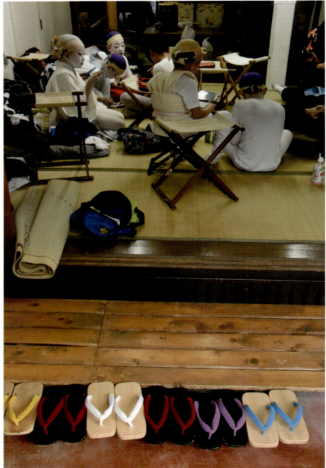

登り山（四月十四日）

昼過ぎから長浜八幡宮へ曳山を曳いて行く。「山送り」ともいう

長浜八幡宮に着くと着帳に記帳
After entering the shrine, a placard on which the float team name and order are written, is placed at the front pillar.

Nobori-Yama (April 14)
The teams pull the festival float to Nagahama Hachimangu from the afternoon. That is also called "Yama-Okuri".

雨天の日は、雨除けシートをかぶって曳行
Even on a rainy day, donning raincoats, the float is pulled through the streets.

曳山の到着を総当番に（右）に報告する山組の負担人ら
The Futan-Nin informs Soutou-Ban of their float's arrival.

曳山後部にのぼりをあげるなど整えて神前入り
Before entering the shrine, the float is arranged by raising the flag at the rear.

先着の山組の若衆たちが、招き扇を振って次に入る山の曳き入れに花を添える
Young members of float teams who have already arrived there wave Manaki-Ogi to provide more fanfare for the next float.

神前入りを済ますと前柱に「席札」を立てる
Even on a rainy day, donning raincoats, the float is pulled through the streets.

74

夕渡り（四月十四日）

山に「灯」が入るころ、御幣とともに役者らが行列を組んで長浜八幡宮から自町へ帰る

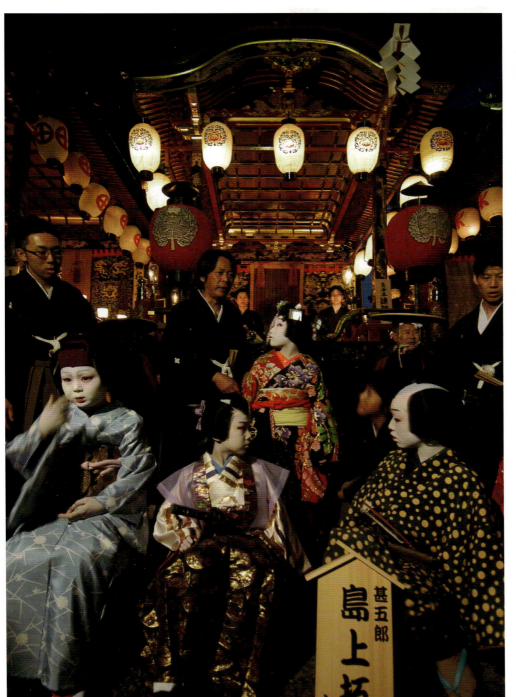

きらびやかな衣装が曳山の灯に映える
Gorgeous costumes look more splendid with the light and shadows cast from lantern lights.

Yu-Watari (April 14)
When the festival floats are illuminated, child Kabuki actors with Gohei make a line to walk home to their own town from Nagahama Hachimangu.

道中、見得を切り、見物客を沸かせる
The audience cheers as a child performer strikes a proud pose.

化粧・着付け

化粧を整え、衣装を着付ける。慌ただしい中、華やかさに包まれる

Costume and make up
When the festival floats are illuminated, child Kabuki actors with Gohei make a line to walk home to their own town from Nagahama Hachimangu.

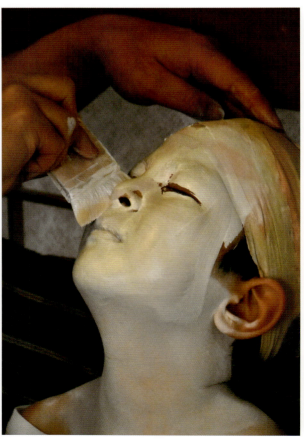
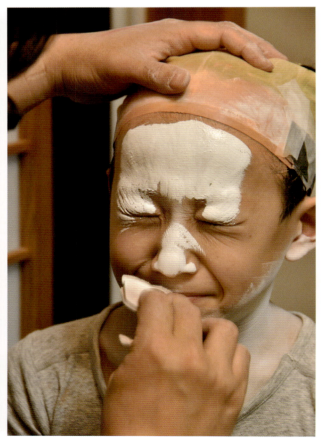

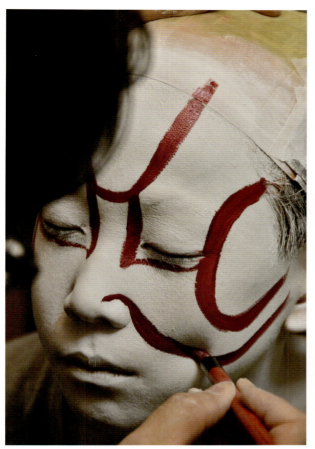

「あーん」。
衣装を汚さないよう、若衆が子ども役者の口にお弁当を運ぶ
"Open your mouth." Young members feed the performers so as not to dirty the costumes.

朝渡り（四月十五日）

本衣装の役者らは、「夕渡り」と逆コースで歩いて長浜八幡宮へ

祭り衣装が古い町並みに溶け込む
The costumes match the traditional town atmosphere.

Asa-Watari (April 15)
Morning parade of child Kabuki actors in costume The Kabuki actors leave for Nagahama Hachimangu, the opposite direction from the "Yu-Watari" of last evening.

猩々丸が出番の時は、奴振りが行列の前につく
 "*Yakkofuri" leads the procession when "Shojo-Maru" is called for their turn in the order of floats.

 *Yakkofuri is a kind of the folk performing art derived from Tomozoroe of samurai family. Tomozoroe are servants who follow a daimyo's procession.

長刀組太刀渡り（四月十五日）

朝渡りの後、御幣を先頭に力士、2メートル余りの太刀を付けた子どもの鎧武者らの一行が長浜八幡宮へ。休息の後、御旅所へ向かう

Naginata-Gumi Tachiwatari (April 15)
 "Asa-Watari", a party of the boys dressed as armoured warriors with 2 meter long swords, go to Nagahama Hachimangu. The procession is led by a young boy carrying the Gohei. After a break, they go to the Otabisho.

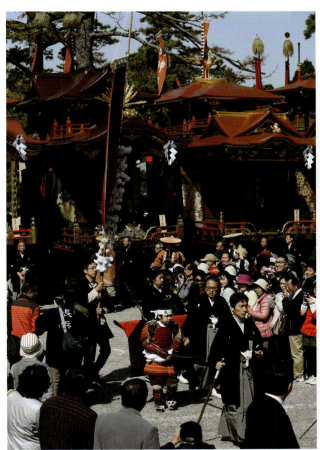

紋付角帯姿に化粧回しをした若衆が
臀部を見せて歩く「しりはしょり」
Young members wear "Montsu-ki-Kakuobi" with ornamental aprons. They roll up the bottoms of their kimono because it is easier for them to walk around. They call the appearance, "Shirihashori".

翁招き（四月十五日）

太刀渡りが境内を出ると、長刀組の裃姿の中老が「最初長刀組」と書いた席札のついた青竹を神前に向かって上下に振り、一番山に差し出す

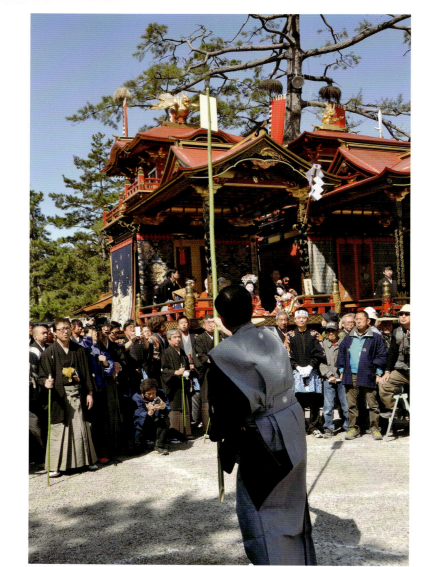

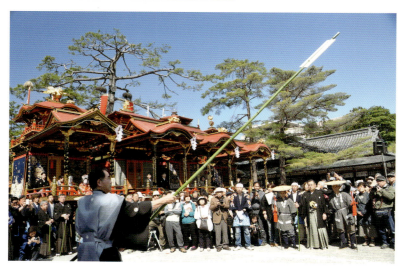

Okina-Maneki (April 15)
After the group of "Tachi-Watari" leave the shrine, one of the warriors waves a long bamboo pole to honor the gods of the shrine. It is given to "Ichiban-Yama", the team which have the first performance of Kabuki play this year.

狂言奉納（四月十五日）

出笛の後、一番山は狂言の幕開けを祝って三番叟を披露。可憐な芸に見物客から大きな拍手がわく

狂言奉納。曳山を奉納場所に曳き出す
The Kabuki play is dedicated to the gods of Nagahama Hachimangu.
The floats are pulled out to the stage.

Kyogen-Hounou (April 15)
After "Debue", the only solo flute song in this festival, "Ichiban-Yama" performs "Sanbaso" by children to celebrate the start of the Kabuki plays. Only Ichiban-Yama is permitted to do it. Sightseers get excited and give a big round of applause for the performances of the children.

狂言の幕開けを祝う「三番叟」。過去は一番山の子どもが舞ったが、現在は公募の子どもが担う
Sanbaso is a Japanese traditional dance of celebration before the Kabuki performance. Until recently it was only performed by children from Ichiban-Yama. Performers are now selected by open auditions and recruitment.

詰めかけた大勢の見物客の前で
熱演が続く
The enthusiastic performance goes on in front of the large crowd that came to see it.

花道を支える若衆たち
Young members support "Hanami-chi", a stage-passage.

道中歌舞伎公演（四月十五日）

狂言奉納が終わった山から御旅所へ。道中、数ヵ所でも歌舞伎を披露する

Do-Chu Kabuki Kouen (April 15)
When the float team finishes performing the Kabuki play in front of god in the shrine, they leave here for the "Otabisho". They also have the public performance of Kabuki play several times at some points along the streets on the way to the "Otabisho"

お旅所神前奉納（四月十五日）

二番山が神前に入るころ日も暮れ、山に灯が入る。照明にきらびやかな衣装が映え、、昼間とは違った風情が

Otabisho Shinzen-Hounou(April 15)

When "Niban-Yama", the second float team, enter the "Otabisho", it is starting to get dark in the evening and the festival floats are lit up to be seen into the night. The beautiful costumes shine brightly by the stage illumination. The festival in the daytime is lovely, of course, however, the beauty of the nighttime is particularly marvelous.

ユネスコ無形文化遺産の登録を記念して、
出番山以外の山も含め十三の全山組の曳山がお旅所に集結
 In commemoration of the designation by UNESCO as an cultural heritage in 2016, all 13 of the float teams get together at the Otabisho.(Usually, only four floats are present here.)

104

長刀組の長刀山と曳山の「灯」の競演
A fantastic collaboration between Naginata-Yama and the lights of other floats.

灯が入り、ひときわ引き立つ舞台。役者たちの演技も艶が増す

The festival floats are lit up to be seen into the night. This creates a beautiful contrast between the illumined actors on floats and the darkness.

神輿還御の儀（四月十五日）
狂言が終わると、神輿が神輿堂から担ぎ出され、本社へと還る

Mikoshi Kangyo no Gi (April 15)
After all of the Kabuki plays are finished, the portable shrine is carried out of the Mikoshi-Dou. It goes back to Nagahama Hachimangu.

戻り山（四月十五日）

神輿が「札の辻」を通過すると、長刀組に続き、一番山から順次曳山は各山組の町内に還る

戻ってきた曳山を提灯で迎える若衆たち
Young members receive the returning float by lantern light.

Modori-Yama (April 15)
After the Mikoshi passes "Huda no Tsuji", a specific street corner, each festival float goes back to their own town in order from "Ichiban-Yama".

子ども歌舞伎観劇会(四月十六日)

「後宴」行事のひとつとして長浜文化芸術会館でも狂言が披露される

Kodomo Kabuki Kangei-Kai (April 16)
A Kabuki play is performed at the Nagahama Culture and Arts Hall (Nagahama Bunka Geijyutsu Kaikan) as one of the events for "Goen".

112

千秋楽(四月十六日)
自町で最後の狂言を披露。若衆ら祭り関係者らは、ホッとすると同時に感慨に深ける

最後の舞台に向かう子ども役者に大きな拍手
The child actors who will perform the last Kabuki play receive great applause from the audience.

Senshuraku; Closing day (April 16)
The teams have the last performance in their own town. Many involved in the festival are overcome by deep emotion as the festivities are coming to a close.

最後の狂言が済むと若衆たちが扇子を振って「ヨイサ、ヨイサ」
After the children finish the last performance, young members call out "Yoisa, yoisa!" and wave fans.

労をねぎらって義太夫ら三役に花束が
Sanyaku including Gidayu get a bunch of flowers as an appreciation for their efforts.

若衆筆頭が次期の筆頭(左)に引き継ぐ
This year's head of young members passes to torch to the leader appointed for next year's festival.

静かに山蔵に入る曳山。感慨深げに見守る若衆たち
The float comes into its house quietly. The young members watching are visibly moved by deep emotion.

御幣返しの儀（四月十七日）
十三日に迎えた御幣を返しに行く。長かった祭りに幕

Gohei Gaeshi no Gi (April 16)
The teams return the Gohei, which they received on the 13th. The long festival has finally come to a close.

山片付け（祭り後）

法被を日干ししたり、中老らが曳山の飾り幕や舞台の障子、外題札などを外して曳山を山蔵へ収める

Cleaning up
Some people dry their "Happi" coats in the sun, others remove the decorations from the floats. After that, the festival float is put back into the "Yamagura", its garage.

120

あとがき

華麗で豪華な山車の舞台で男児が歌舞伎を演じる長浜曳山まつり。出会いは、私が長浜に赴任した昭和四七年春。とある山組の稽古場を訪ねたときからだ。

仮舞台で、子どもたちが振付師の指導で狂言を習っていた。武家言葉独特の台詞を、もどかしそうにしゃべる。振付師の所作を懸命に覚えようとする。振付師から時に、厳しい声が飛ぶ。悔し涙を浮かべる子ども役者。最初は、写真を撮るのも忘れて稽古を見守った。

ぎこちなかった子どもたちも練習を重ねるうちに様になってくる。女型は艶めかしく、武士役は凛とした男役になっていく。春休みのわずか三週間ほどで狂言を身につける。

祭りの中心的な役割を担う若衆の働きぶりにも感心した。一月から役割を決める「初寄り」やパンフレット作り、稽古が始まるとつきっきりで子ども役者の送り迎えなど身の回りの世話をする。お茶汲み、後片付け…と普段家庭ではしない雑用も黙々とこなしながら祭りを支える。

最初は「立ち稽古」、「裸参り」、「籤取り式」、「登り山」、「夕渡り」、「狂言奉納」…と祭りの表舞台ばかりを撮影。若衆や中老らと話しをしているうちに四百年の伝統の重さ、支える苦労が分かってきた。と、同時に少子高齢化による振付師、子ども役者の減少など深刻な問題や一部で行事が簡素化されようとしていることも分かった。「いまのうちに、記録として残さなければいけない」。祭りの奥深く踏み入れて撮影する決心をした。幸い、寛容で他人に寄り添う気持ちの強い土地柄か、毎年、山組が協力してくれた。

122

山組によってしきたりも違う。この場面もあの場面も撮りたい。撮影は6年間続いた。完全な記録をしたいと思ったとき、転勤の辞令が出た。完全ではないが、昭和五四年春に写真集にして出版した。

退職した平成十九年。三十年ぶりに滋賀県に帰ってきた。長浜を離れている間に祭りに大きな変化があった。長浜市曳山博物館の完成をきっかけに「曳山交替式」という新しい行事が誕生。振付や太夫、三味線の後継者を育てる長浜曳山文化協会の「三役修業塾」が立ち上げられ、三役を地元の人たちで支えている山組もある。狂言を祝う「三番叟」の子役を公募するようにもなった。

減少している若衆や子ども役者にも変化が。山組以外の地区に住む住民が若衆や子ども役者として参加、山組に溶け込み祭りを盛り上げている。囃子（しゃぎり）も友好のある山組同士が助け合うなど関係者らは知恵を絞って伝統行事を守り続けている。そういった姿を見て、私自身を鼓舞しながら再び撮影を続けさせてもらっている。

最初の写真集は、祭りが国の重要無形文化財に指定されたときに出版、今回はユネスコの無形文化遺産に登録されて間もなく出版することができた。今後も微力ながら伝統を守っていく手助けになればと撮影していきたい。

出版に際し、長浜曳山まつりについて寄稿して頂いた長浜曳山文化協会理事の西川丈雄さんはじめ、取材協力してくださった川地岳志さん、翻訳を担当してくださった奥様の米亜さん、英語の監修をお願いしたポップ・ベンジャミンさん、撮影に協力してくださった山組、まつり関係者、出版に尽力して頂いた能美舎の堀江昌史さんら皆様にお礼申し上げます。

平成三十一年三月　吉川宏暉

写真・解説　吉川宏暉（よしかわ・ひろあき）
1972年3月　　長浜市に赴任
1975年春　　　本格的に長浜曳山まつりを撮影
1978年9月　　岡山県津山市に転任
1979年2月　　長浜曳山まつりが国の「重要無形文化財」に指定される
1979年3月　　「長浜曳山まつり－こども歌舞伎」を出版
2007年9月　　退職。滋賀県に居住
2008年4月　　全日本写真連盟に入会。再び、長浜曳山まつりの撮影を再開

訳者　　川地米亜（かわち・まいあ）
昭和54年生まれ。神戸市出身。関西学院大総合政策学部総合政策学科卒。
大手外資系メーカー勤務。退職後、長浜へ移住。現在、フリーランサーとして
webライティングや英語翻訳などを請け負う。
英語翻訳では、北町組青海山発行の長浜曳山まつりパンフレット（一部）。

英語監修　Benjamin Popp
取材協力　青海山若衆　川地岳志（かわち・たけし）
　　　　　各山組、曳山関係者の皆さん

こども歌舞伎　長浜曳山まつり

2019年3月初版発行
著　者　吉川宏暉
装　丁　安藤克也（AMATA）
発行者　堀江昌史
印刷所　シナノ印刷
発行所　能美舎
　　　　滋賀県長浜市木之本町大音1017
　　　　丘峰喫茶店内
　　　　電話(0749)82-5066
　　　　http://www.kyuhokissaten.com

ISBN 978-4-909-62301-0
定価1800円+税